This Hope Remains

A Story of Staying Through the Storms

Christi Rogers Gibson

Your Story Matters Books

Title: This Hope Remains

A Story Of Staying Through The Storms

By Christi Rogers Gibson

Paperback 979-8-9907436-0-1

Ebook 979-8-9907436-1-8

To the dear friends and family
who have accompanied me on this journey.
You're my people.
You continued to serve with me.
You let me continue to serve with you.
You ate ice cream and snowballs,
made me laugh, and cried with me.
You encouraged me to take the next step
and never called me crazy—at least not out loud.
You called, stopped by, or sent a card or text for no reason.
You helped me get through an hour, a day, or a season.
You found me where I was, whether in the pit, on the ledge,
or eager to share a breakthrough—and you pulled me out,
talked me down, and rejoiced with me.
You were God's new mercies each morning.
I needed you. I still do.

To the listeners and the readers.
You've heard it all. More than once.
You've told me when my words made no sense
and when they came out wrong.
Some of you took out commas and others put them in.
You all helped me breathe. God used you to write my story.
And you told me it mattered.

To my stops along the way.
I'm grateful for your driveways and plug-ins,
your guest rooms, your tables,
and most of all for your time.
You are the strength and mutual encouragement
that keeps me on the road.

To my dad, my mom, and my sister.
It hasn't always been easy.
We didn't always understand each other.
But you've always been there for me,
even when it was hard.
I am who I am because of you.

To Judi and Allen.
You came when I called.
You took over when I just couldn't.
You let go when I needed to fly or fail.
You took me home with you and you let me stay.

To Callie and Trey
We were a party of four
and became a party of three together.
We felt all the feels. We cried.
We laughed. We forgave.

We endured. Together.
You let me tell your story,
stopped me when I told too much,
forgave me when you couldn't stop me,
and encouraged me to tell more when I was afraid.
You made us a party of seven
and my heart is full because of you.
No mother could be more blessed by her children
and the grown-up people they've become.
I love you.

Table of Contents

Introduction

My world came crashing down on August 24, 2015.

In the years since that fateful day, the sorrow remains but the pain has dulled. Distance has provided perspective. From this vantage point, I see the reason for the hope I held on to for almost thirty years and the hope I cling to today.

This is my hope story.

I cannot tell my husband's story. I don't know what he was thinking, what he wanted, or why he did what he did. I don't even know all of his words and actions. For me to know his perspective is impossible, I can only guess.

Yet, I can't completely untangle my story from his, so it's inevitable that in telling mine, I'll tell some of his. How his story looked from my view.

John Gibson was more than one thing—more complicated than just a name on a website or even my understanding of him. I'll do my best to honor him without protecting an image.

My hope story is not about dealing with suicide or sexual addiction. Both topics are a part of my story, so I will talk about the impact both had on my hope. If you have experienced a suicide or struggle with thoughts of suicide, please know there are effective resources and tools for you. Talk to your pastor or a trusted friend or counselor.

If you don't have a local connection, the suicide hotline, 988, is always available to anyone.

If you feel hopeless and think of harming yourself, please call 911 or get to your local hospital emergency room for immediate assistance.

This is my hope story. And it's God's story. I can't tell my story without telling you about God and his ways. His book, the Bible, is written so we can know who God is, his character, and the ways God works in us and for us. His story continues to play out in our stories.

This is not a how-to book. There are no step-by-step instructions. Perhaps reading my story will somehow help you to understand your own.

This story starts with a girl who wanted to make rainbows. She traveled down a winding road where that girl became a woman who lived in a van by the river. At every stop, I believe you'll find glimpses of a hope.

I hope you interact. Make a total mess of this book. In the margins jot a big, "Me too!" or "No way!" or "What?" Scribble your responses, notes, additions, and even corrections on every page. If you do make a mess, please take a photo and send the picture to me in an email.

I'd love to see how messy this book can get.

Chapter One

Naked

"But do not overlook this one fact, beloved, that with the Lord one day is as a thousand years, and a thousand years as one day. The Lord is not slow to fulfill his promise as some count slowness, but is patient toward you, not wishing that any should perish, but that all should reach repentance. But the day of the Lord will come like a thief, and then the heavens will pass away with a roar, and the heavenly bodies will be burned up and dissolved, and the earth and the works that are done on it will be exposed," 2 Peter 3:8-10 ESV.

"Life is short, have an affair." The advertisement promised complete anonymity to anyone who used their site to make secret connections.

God could have allowed John's addiction to be discovered quietly. We'd seen other ministers resign and disappear. There had been rumors and speculation, but no one knew for sure why they had left.

All it would have required was for one computer guy to discover pornography on my husband's computer and we could have escaped only slightly scathed.

But God had bigger plans.

On August 24, 2015, John's name was only one among millions registered on the Ashley Madison website for cheating spouses. Hackers broke through the site's weak security system and released a list of clients who trusted the empty promise that their information would be safe. John's secret life was exposed. Carefully built and protected, his image shattered in an instant.

When the hidden facts became public, John was confronted. He expressed his regrets and signed a letter of resignation.

Unaware of the sudden events that changed our lives forever, I left work that day and drove home. Coming inside, I found my husband. He was dead by suicide.

Image. It takes a lifetime to build and only a moment to demolish. My image was gone, I was left standing naked and alone in its rubble.

The hackers who released millions of names registered on a website for cheating spouses had no idea who I was. They had my husband's name on their list but I was not on their radar.

They didn't know how painstakingly I had constructed and maintained my image as the wife of a pastor and seminary professor. Their actions had irreparable consequences. The life I protected for so long was over.

Difficult Conversations

We lived in a loving community. A precious team of friends sat at my dining room table and located pastors and friends to be on standby when I spoke to my kids. I did not want them to be alone when they heard the news or to drive by themselves to New Orleans.

My house and front yard were filled with people who loved us. The backyard was empty, quiet, and dark. So that was where I went to make the calls that only I could make. I went to the middle of the yard, outside the circle of light coming from inside. I bent low to the grass, and curled in on myself—one arm wrapped tightly around my knees and the other clutching the phone as I fumbled through the words.

Telling my children their dad died by suicide was the hardest thing I've ever done. I don't remember what I said. I know I came right out with the facts with no preliminaries or build-up.

I told my children. My sister. John's brother and sister. But I let our siblings tell our parents so they would receive the news in person instead of by phone. Despite my seminary course on Death, Loss, and Grief, nothing prepared me for this.

My friends had called 911 and made all the arrangements. They patiently walked with me through everything that had to be done. I did only those things that only I could do. The rest of the time, I sat frozen on the couch. One friend coaxed me to eat and hand-fed me finger sandwiches.

Our friends expressed confusion and shock. They didn't yet know what I knew about his addiction. They had no context for understanding his suicide.

Once my children and I were in the same room, we agreed, "No more lies."

It turns out, John and I hadn't kept our secrets from these precious two who lived with us. Both had been unwilling witnesses to our secret-keeping and image-building.

My children and I were broken and beyond exhausted. We hated that John was gone, but we could not bear to continue in the lies. Longing for freedom, we would have preferred to be free with him, but we would no longer keep the lie without him.

There was no way to imagine what freedom this decision to speak the truth and walk in light would give. Nor could I guess the price this resolve would require. Even though the phrases felt uncomfortable, I began to say aloud the words *suicide* and *sexual addiction*.

Your Turn

The Naked Dream was my recurring nightmare for years. As I walked down the hallway at school, at church, or in the office, suddenly I realized I am naked. Variations of the dream included being partially dressed but missing essential items like my pants or a top.

It doesn't take a degree in psychology to realize the source of this nightmare. I was afraid of being seen.

Psalm 139:1-8 ESV says:
> "You have searched me, Lord, and you know me.
> You know when I sit and when I rise;
> you perceive my thoughts from afar.
> You discern my going out and my lying down;
> you are familiar with all my ways.
> Before a word is on my tongue you,
> Lord, know it completely.
> You hem me in behind and before,
> and you lay your hand upon me.
> Such knowledge is too wonderful for me,
> too lofty for me to attain."

Do these verses feel promising or threatening to you?

Are there parts of you that you would rather not be known? Your thoughts? The places you go? How you rest? Your ways? Your words?

Do you long to be surrounded by God, or are there times you'd rather he stay out of your business? Is his knowledge wonderful to you?

Take a minute to respond honestly to these words written thousands of years ago.

Chapter Two

Pollyanna Power

"And most generally there is something about everything that you can be glad about, if you keep hunting long enough to find it."—— Pollyanna Whittier, in *Pollyanna* by Eleanor H. Porter

In one of my earliest memories, my family was in the car on the way to church. Daddy was a part-time music leader and a full-time school principal. Mama was a school librarian during the week and taught kids in the youth group on Sundays. Life was busy and getting our family out of the house on Sunday mornings was stressful.

Based on where I picture this memory, I couldn't have been older than six. My mama and daddy argued in the front seat while my sister and I tried to be inconspicuous in the back seat. This memory has no soundtrack so I don't know what the fight was about. I remember Mama cried and Daddy's ears turned that reddish-purple hue that screams caution. Daddy said something, probably sarcastic, and Mama hit him.

Overshadowing the whole memory is the overwhelming sense of personal responsibility I felt. Somehow that little girl in the back seat thought that if she could be agreeable and peaceful enough she could make her Daddy's anger and Mama's worry go away.

No one taught me to put my hope in positive thinking. Yet somehow, I bought into the idea. I have always sought to be the positive one at the table. I had an incredible inspiration for the role I wanted to play—her name was Pollyanna Whittier.

The Disney movie, *Pollyanna*, based on Eleanor Porter's book series by the same name, released the year before I was born. This was pre-VHS days, so I'm not sure when I first saw the film but I played my positive role long before I discovered Hayley Mills as the orphaned child of missionary parents who changes an entire town.

In the movie, the recently orphaned Pollyanna comes to live with her only surviving relative, an aunt who had never married or had children of her own. Aunt Polly was a curmudgeon—a particular sort of ill-tempered person who had become set in her ways. Pollyanna's positivity quickly makes an impact on everyone she meets. Eventually, her approach softens her aunt's heart. The transformed Aunt Polly reunites with her long-lost love.

Rainbows On The Wall

In my favorite scene, Pollyanna barges into the home of another curmudgeon, Mr. Pendergast, and discovers a rainbow on his wall. The source of the colors is sunshine refracted through a crystal pendant on a light fixture. She later returns with Jimmy Bean, the town urchin, and the two children string glass pieces from Mr. Pendergast's lamps and chandeliers to create rainbows on the walls throughout his spacious home. Mr. Pendergast, Jimmy Bean, and Pollyanna are all glad. Later, the former curmudgeon adopts the former urchin, and Mr. Pendergast and Jimmy Bean also live happily ever after. Again, this makes the whole town, including Pollyanna, glad.

I have a soft spot in my heart for curmudgeons, especially the ones in this story. I wanted to be Pollyanna. I wanted to create rainbows and make the whole town glad. I knew that if I only had Pollyanna Power, I could be the crystal that made rainbows on the wall. I could change my family. Probably the world. No one would be mad or sad anymore. We would all be glad.

I still believe in being positive. I'm a GiGi who always attempts to cheer grumpy toddlers with an Itsy Bitsy Spider arm tickle, a game of peekaboo, or a silly, made-up song with their names included. I'm convinced that if I first change my face, a change in my attitude will follow. Surely speaking the truth aloud can regulate my emotional response to tough circumstances.

Positivity can change attitudes or emotions.

The Bible says in Proverbs 17:12 that "a joyful heart is good medicine." The physical act of smiling releases dopamine, endorphins, and serotonin in the body. These hormones can improve mood.

Positivity alone does not bring about lasting change. When my grandson is unhappy to have his diaper changed, I can make him giggle with a song. Especially, when that song has motions with it. But even if his fussing turns to smiles, the mess is still there, and the diaper needs to be removed. He needs to be cleaned and a new diaper put in place. Anything else is unhealthy. And stinky.

Rainbow Maker

No one can make the whole world glad. A little girl can't change the dynamics of her family. The grown-ups in her life are supposed to provide a nurturing environment for her. Even big people need to rely on Someone bigger than themselves. But I didn't know that then. The feelings I felt that day in the car shaped my understanding of my place in the world for far too long.

In my childish mind, the way to make people glad was to make them like me. To make them like me, I reasoned, was to become more of what they liked and less of what they didn't like. If I couldn't become more or less, I would fake it.

I learned to cover my faults and exaggerate my virtues. I became a storyteller and much of what I told would have fit best into the fiction genre.

Pollyanna wasn't my only role model. Nancy Drew, Laura Ingalls Wilder, and Heidi were favorites, too. When we visited my grandparents at their home, I read and reread their stacks of Reader's Digest magazines and a well-loved set of heavy books filled with fairy tales.

Our church library had biographies for children that I read when fiction was unavailable. Real people were flawed, and I preferred my hero to be always good, always right, and to always win in the end. God created me in his image, but I constructed a new image that I thought was better.

A Place For Rainbows

My image wasn't completely fiction like Pollyanna or Heidi, but more like Laura Ingalls Wilder—not entirely historical, but loosely based on a true story. And my image made rainbows.

There is a place for rainbows. They come after a storm and symbolize hope and promise. The first rainbow was created by a good God who loves us enough to provide a refuge from destruction. He placed a rainbow in the sky to remind us of his faithfulness. It's a symbol. A good and beautiful symbol.

Reliance on Pollyanna Power put my hope in my ability to generate the rainbow myself rather than in the God who is the source of all hope. I settled for a rainbow on the wall instead of rejoicing in the Creator of the rainbow in the sky.

While I made rainbows, my husband grew up as the middle child of a Southern Baptist preacher and a high school English teacher.

John competed in sports, had a paper route, and read many of the same books I did. Like me, he found many of his titles in the church library. His favorite books were the Hardy Boys.

John's dad had reached manhood in the belly of a bomber plane during World War II. The experience had hardened the man. John often spoke of trying and failing to please his dad.

One definition of hope is the confident expectation of future good. Does Pollyanna Power fit this definition? Does making rainbows produce a hope that remains?

I was confident in my rainbow-making skills because they carried me through much of my childhood. I expected them to bring good. But they weren't enough. There were always curmudgeons who would not be charmed by rainbows and gladness.

Mr. Pendergast

I was surprised when some people found my positivity and rainbows irritating.

When I was on a church staff, my feelings were hurt by a Mr. Pendergast-like church member who I could not make like me, no matter how hard I tried or how big I smiled.

My pastor assured me that this man didn't like anyone.

"I want everyone to like me," I said to my pastor.

He laughed. "Oh, Christi, a lot of people don't like you."

His words were a kindness—a wake-up that freed me from the impossible responsibility to please all the people all the time. If only I could remember and live in that freedom.

I could never make everyone glad. There would always be people with pain larger than my rainbows on the wall. When faced with the complicated grief of my broken marriage and my husband's suicide, I lost the ability to make rainbows altogether.

I learned that Pollyanna's rainbows and my rainbows were insufficient and temporary.

Your Turn

My mom had a bright yellow poster in our kitchen that asked a question in bold pink and red graphics, "Will it matter that I was?"

In my mind, I mattered only if I made people happy. I measured my success by my ability to turn a frown upside down.

What impact do you want to have on the world around you? What makes you matter?

Chapter Three

Romantic Notions

It is a truth universally acknowledged, that a single man in possession of a good fortune, must be in want of a wife. — *Pride And Prejudice* by Jane Austen

I had just aged into double digits and blue jeans when the Jesus Revolution arrived in Iowa. In the early 70s our family lived in a suburb of Des Moines called Urbandale.

My friends and I dove into the revolution with all the enthusiasm of nerdy prepubescent girls in love with the idea of love, but completely grossed out by boys. We focused all of our romantic dreams on Jesus. It's okay to laugh at us. I laugh too when I recall how I doodled his name for hours, practicing first on plain white notebook paper, then carefully transferring my designs to special, printed paper. I drew *One Way* arrows, ichthus fish, hearts, and wrote I LUV Jesus; Jesus + Christi = LUV; Jesus is LUV.

Love was a Sunday School word. But LUV was revolutionary.

Interestingly, I don't remember drawing crosses in any of my doodling. Maybe crosses weren't groovy enough.

Around this time, my reading shifted from brave girl stories to romantic novels. My hopes and longings for a relationship changed as well. I dreamed less about rainbows and more about fireworks.

Our family moved back to Texas when I was in my early teens. I visited the local used bookstore with my mom on the first day of summer vacation to stock up on books for the lazy days ahead. I made a beeline for the romance aisle, where I spent the next hour scanning the back covers of books to find just the right love stories to cuddle up with at home. The store had a policy that the more books a customer purchased, the cheaper the books cost, so I usually left with more than one hundred books. The stack provided about a month of reading and then mom and I returned to the bookstore to purchase more titles.

With romance on my mind, I bought into the storyline that there was a boy somewhere who was just waiting to meet my eyes across a crowded room and fall in love with me. Although I knew I'd probably never meet a reclusive English lord of the manor, or his Scottish counterpart, or a dashing laird of the castle like the women in the novels I read, I expected my life to follow the basic outline of the typical romance story.

Mystery Man

My mystery man and I would meet serendipitously and be inexplicably drawn together. Our love would be hindered by insurmountable chasms and thwarted by conflict, but we'd triumph over all obstacles—knowing we were the very essence of life for each other. I got my vocabulary from those romance novels.

The girl who wanted to make everyone glad and impress them with her works, now longed to be cherished. I wanted to be essential to someone.

The stories I read weren't sexually explicit. I viewed some soft pornography at a friend's house when I was young, but any ideas I had about sexual intimacy were fed more by movies than anything else. These films and my romantic reading stirred a desire and shaped my expectations for marriage.

My dream husband and I would be of one heart and one mind. He would always desire only me, and I would always desire only him. We might fight, but making up would come quickly and inevitably take us to a new level of trust and intimacy. None of this seemed unreasonable to me at all.

While I voraciously consumed romance novels, John's hopes for intimacy were similarly being shaped.

I don't know all of what he experienced, but he did tell me he'd had access to adult magazines and developed a habit of viewing pornography at an early age. Before we married, he defended some of what he looked at—like the soft pornography of swimsuit calendars. Though troubled by his stance, I didn't feel confident enough to argue.

The Romance Begins

I can talk about my growth and development firsthand, and I've made some assumptions about John's experience. When John and I met in our mid-20s, we were both far more ordinary than the characters we had fantasized about.

John was a seminary student. I worked in the school system as a Speech Pathologist and commuted to grad school one night each week. We had several commonalities. We'd both grown up in middle-class, church-going families who valued education.

Our faith was at the center of our lives and important to us both. He was studying to be a preacher, and my people thought I'd make a great preacher's wife. We checked off many of the items on one another's checklist for a future spouse. We seemed like a good fit.

Additionally, there a chasm for us to overcome. Though not insurmountable enough to be worthy of a romance novel or Hallmark movie, the challenge seemed to me to be a little romantic. John was Louisiana-born, Georgia-raised, Mississippi-educated, and living in New Orleans. He was pure Southern, through and through.

Texas-born, Texas-raised, Texas-educated, and living in Texas, I was pure Texan.

Texas Proud

I'd always thought of Texas as southern. But I soon learned there is the South and there is Texas. "You can always tell a Texan," John joked. "You just can't tell them much."

While I'll admit Texans are obnoxiously Texas proud, any time spent with a fan of an SEC team will confirm Southerners are obnoxious, too. I naively thought the distance between North Texas and New Orleans was the biggest chasm we had to cross. In our pre-cellular days, we paid long-distance rates to talk on the phone. One of us had to drive or fly 650 miles one way to see each other. We made great sacrifices to be together but, when we were in the same place, we had a few days of concentrated time to focus only on each other.

We wrote letters that took several days to arrive, delivered through the United States Postal Service. Each handwritten letter filled with longing was romantic.

A prolific letter writer, John excelled in this part of our relationship. John saved all of the letters he received as well as the early drafts of letters he wrote. The process of writing, addressing, and putting something in the mail felt tedious to me, but I was highly motivated to exchange letters with John. I felt that John and I said things in our letters that we never would have spoken in person. Words were carefully chosen until it seemed like we used a different vocabulary.

The letters were intense. I'd read what he wrote to me over and over. I read between the lines, adjusting my tone of voice with each reading, imagining what he didn't say along with what he said. I only stopped reading one letter when the next one arrived in the mail. Sometimes I pulled out the whole box of his letters I carefully saved and binge-read through them all. The distance between us created waiting, longing, sacrifice, and miscommunication. All the makings of a good, exciting, and mysterious romance.

Missed Messages

Focused on overcoming the challenge of distance, I missed many of the important challenges that should have been obvious. Our common bond of being church kids blinded me to our disparate family cultures. I was spoiled; he was self-sufficient. I was enmeshed with my family; he was more independent. I told my family everything; he told his family very little.

We shared a faith as well as many of our views on marriage, yet my dream of how faith and marriage would look in practice turned out to be different than his expectations. Because our visits were monthly weekend intensives, I easily missed concerns I might have noticed if we saw each other daily.

I imagined marriage would be like our letters. Surely when we were together we would talk even more and share our deepest thoughts. What I didn't realize in those early days was that John's love language was acts of service. John consistently declared his expectation that our love would be expressed through doing and serving. Trust and intimacy, if even necessary, would probably take care of themselves.

Serving was a part of his romantic dream and what he chose to talk about in his toast at our rehearsal dinner. True love, he said, would be he and I always trying to out-do one another with acts of service. When he said it, it sounded almost romantic.

Most importantly, we had different views on faithfulness and fidelity. While neither of us had been cloistered, I thought we had similar levels of sexual experience. We both said that we'd saved ourselves for marriage.

I dreamed of the fun we'd share learning intimacy, and hoped we'd only grow to enjoy each other more over the years. In reality, John already had an appetite for variety that I could never satisfy and he would grow tired of me quickly.

We were both full of romantic hopes and dreams. They were just different.

Your Turn

What has shaped your dreams for romance?

What makes you feel loved and cherished?

Have your hopes been fulfilled or disappointed?

Chapter Four

I Think I Can

I think I can. I think I can. I think I can. Up, up, up. Faster and faster and faster and faster the little engine climbed until at last they reached the top of the mountain. — Watty Piper, *The Little Engine That Could*

Afternel John's death, I faced the task of cleaning out John's office.

I don't think I'm exaggerating when I call my husband a hoarder of paper.

He had ten four-drawer filing cabinets crammed full of all types of documents. The floor-to-ceiling bookshelves that lined all four walls overflowed and papers were stuffed between the books. Even the books had papers between their pages. File boxes packed with paper were stacked on top of every bookcase.

In desperate need of legal and financial information, my children and I felt obligated to go through paper by paper. We also wanted to find anything that could help his church and the seminary finish his work.

Most of all, we wanted to understand him.

Blessings and Pain

So we forced open the overstuffed drawers, dug through the reams, scanned the spiral notebooks, flipped through the files, and considered the calendars. We read and read.

After sharing the heartbreaking news of their father's death with my children, this process was the second hardest task I've ever done. Occasionally I still relive the trauma of some of the discoveries that were made during those days.

There were blessings among the pain. And even some healing laughter. We stopped to celebrate every time we found another stack of copies of one particular treasure stuck into a file. The gift that kept giving, I wish we had counted. There were more than one hundred copies among John's papers of a particular poem.

Titled *Thinking* by Walter D. Wintle, John used the poem in sermons, classes, and motivational speeches. We figured he made the copies because he wanted to be ready to share the composition with anyone who asked where they could find it.

The poem explains a lot about John. He was a doer who thought he could power through anything with the strength of his will.

Written in 1902, the wording of some of this piece may seem odd, yet the poem has stood the test of time. The composition certainly meant a great deal to John. After a rough day, John came across a tract in his locker room with the printed poem. The impact of Wintle's poem on John was life-changing.

Frequently, John spoke of sharing the poem with a friend who was contemplating suicide. John said the message saved his life.

Thinking

by Walter D. Wintle

If you think you are beaten, you are

If you think you dare not, you don't,

If you like to win, but you think you can't

It is almost certain you won't.

If you think you'll lose, you're lost

For out of the world we find,

Success begins with a fellow's will

It's all in the state of mind.

If you think you are outclassed, you are

You've got to think high to rise,

You've got to be sure of yourself before

You can ever win a prize.

Life's battles don't always go
To the stronger or faster man,
But soon or late the man who wins
Is the man who thinks he can.
Published in 1905
Unity Tract Society, Unity School of Christianity

My husband was the quintessential *Little Engine Who Could*. He accomplished much that was beyond his ability simply because he thought he could.

John was known for his willingness to work on car repairs for free. At any given time, I could find a car in our driveway that he'd taken apart and would soon put back together.

A student would ask, "Can you..."

Without hesitation, John replied, "Yes."

If he didn't know how to fix a problem, he ordered the car's manual and searched how-to videos until he figured out what was needed. When he was stumped, John consulted with a few professional mechanics. I don't remember any projects he gave up on.

John experienced quite a bit of success with his *I think I can* attitude toward life. But while that attitude can masquerade as hope, it is not a hope that remains.

Works and Image

One of my favorite passages of Scripture ends with this word of attribution to God. "Now to him who is able to do far more abundantly than all that we ask or think, according to the power at work within us, to him be glory in the church and in Christ Jesus throughout all generations, forever and ever. Amen," Ephesians 3:20-21 ESV.

Do you see the difference between Wintle's lauding the man who thinks he can and Paul's words giving glory to the God who is able? Success that begins with a fellow's will is nothing like a hope that is "according to God's power at work in us."

"The man who wins is the man who thinks he can," does not rely on a God "who is able to do far more abundantly than all that we ask or think. "Wintle's poem is about works. Wintle's poem is image.

In the end, both works and image will fail. So will dreams.

I was a dreamer with expectations of happy endings. I knew bad things could happen to me, but illness would always be healed and disagreements would always be resolved. People, especially my husband, might stray, but he would always love me in the end.

John was a doer, with the confident expectation that there was nothing he couldn't power through.

He was also an addict. His compulsive thoughts and behaviors controlled his life and destroyed our marriage. Addiction is not overcome by thinking you can or dreaming of an addiction-free life.

I believe misplacing his hope in his ability to power through contributed to John's suicide. His hope in his own strength failed him when he felt most desperate.

Your Turn

Do you sometimes feel stuck in a perpetual version of the *Bear Hunt* song from childhood? In the song, the bear hunters encounter one obstacle after another that they can't go over or around. They declared they are not scared, and now they must power through to the end.

How has a can-do attitude worked out for you?

Has an I-think-I-can mindset ever failed you?

Is there something you face today that you cannot power through?

Chapter Five

Secrets in the Attic

"But when anything is exposed by the light, it becomes visible, for anything that becomes visible is light. Therefore it says, "Awake, O sleeper, and arise from the dead, and Christ will shine on you," Ephesians 5:13-14 ESV.

I was passing through town, and on a whim, decided to drive by a home my husband and I had shared in a previous season of life. I parked across the street and sat in my car remembering birthday parties for our children, Christmas celebrations, and the time my daughter found a snake in her backyard sandbox.

Then my stomach wrenched as I recalled a moment in the attic of that house. I hadn't thought of this memory in a while, but viewing the front of the house, the picture came clearly.

I don't remember what I was looking for when I climbed those stairs to the attic. But I remember how I felt when I found the box.

There are moments vividly fixed in our minds and so significant they become a point from which we order time. We speak in terms of before and after these instances when everything changed. Flashbulb memories mark births or deaths, a first kiss or when trust was broken. I remember minute details as if looking at a photo of the flashbulb moment that rocked my marriage.

A young wife with a few nagging worries about my marriage, I repeatedly brushed aside the concerns that nibbled at my thoughts. I mostly blamed my own insecurities and my husband's work pressures for anything that seemed missing from our life together. I expected that our relationship would get better. We would be okay. If not today, then surely tomorrow.

Forever Changed

In the attic, I opened a box of seemingly random trash, and sorted through, thinking I'd throw the contents away. There were bank statements, bills, and other financial records that made no sense to me. Then, with a shock, I realized this was not trash at all. The information was hugely significant.

My eyes were opened as my understanding of the situation dawned. Life would never be okay again. My expectations, assumptions, and perceptions of my marriage and my husband were forever changed. The young, hopeful woman who had climbed those stairs no longer existed. Instantly, I felt old, tired, and in that moment, hopeless.

John and I would experience many moments of truth in the years after that trip to the attic. My discovery that day would not be the most difficult in my marriage. But it was the first. And the new awareness rocked my world.

It's been more than thirty years, and I can still feel the roughness of the attic floorboards where I sat as I made the terrible discovery. I can hear the attic ladder creak, feel the rail under my hand, and the tremble in my legs as I climbed down to the hallway. The ache in my gut has become an all too familiar, though unwelcome, companion for years to come.

Vivid Memory

The memory is vivid because the trajectory of my life changed in a moment. This fresh realization suddenly provided unwanted answers to the questions that had pressed against my days. This wake-up call didn't interrupt a dream as much as introduced a nightmare.

I was a woman I had never expected to be, living in a place where I never thought I would go. Worse, I knew I was married to a man I did not know.

There was no divorce in our families. John was a pastor. Pastors don't divorce. It does not fit the image.

In the months after the trip to the attic, John and I sought counseling. It was the one and only time we did that in our 29-year marriage because counseling meant being seen. Counseling could destroy our image, but so would divorce. We chose counseling. We decided to try professional help before we talked about divorce.

However, even in the privacy of the counseling room, image won over honest confession.

In one session we argued for the full hour about how one of us still loved the other, but didn't like them, while one of us still liked, but no longer loved the other. I honestly cannot remember which was me and which was John. The fruitless effort seemed such a waste of time for the counselor and for us.

After driving for more than an hour to meet with this counselor, ostensibly to save our marriage, we could not talk to him about the main reason we were considering an end. That was the last time we sought counseling together.

We stayed married for another eighteen years.

Living A Lie

The mental and physical exhaustion of living a lie and maintaining our image eventually forced John to step away from his pastorate.

He decided to spend an intensive week at a well-respected in-patient clinic.

At the end of the week, I was invited to a couples' session with his counselor. We weren't far into our hour together before I realized John was repeating the same pattern we experienced in our previous counseling. John had talked about issues with his dad. He had talked about issues with me. But he had not shared the most relevant issue that caused the most destruction.

When the counselor asked what I thought about something John had said, I responded, "How is all of this related to my husband's infidelity?"

The counselor shot a questioning look at John. John confirmed what I'd said was true.

"John," the counselor said, "we're going to need another week."

John and I paid a licensed counselor and then an entire team of mental health professionals, all legally and morally bound to confidentiality, to help us. We rearranged our lives to get their help. Then we sabotaged their ability to provide help by not being honest about our lives and our struggles.

We were in trouble. But we hid our desperation in a dark corner of our precious image and moved on.

Why Stay?

Eventually, we decided to stay together. We agreed we'd work through some books on marriage together.

We decided to fix our problems ourselves.

While we were working through a book called *His Needs, Her Needs*, John said he had no needs. No needs. At all. Working to fix things meant something different to him than it did to me.

Why did we stay? Did we have hope? The answers to those questions are complicated. The day in the attic, the attempts at counseling, and the self-help books were all a part of my hope journey. Looking back, I think there were three main reasons I stayed.

- I liked the image I'd built. I enjoyed being seen as a pastor's wife, a Bible teacher, and a woman of prayer. By now, we had the perfect happy family: one husband, one wife, one daughter, and one son. I wanted to keep my life because viewed from the outside looking in, this image was the story I'd expected to live. When John and I talked about losing everything, my pride in my image provided staying power.

- I was afraid. My confidence was at an all-time low. If my husband did not love me, I reasoned that this proved I must be unlovable. Everyone loved John. I might not get custody of my children in a divorce, and even if I did, I was afraid I wasn't capable of raising them alone. Fear drove me.

- I hoped. In my mind, I created a dream story about how God would use this time in our lives. He would heal our marriage. We would share our journey and God would give us a ministry of helping others restore their marriages. We would love each other once more and live happily ever after. I had a lasting hope in God, diluted by the hope I placed in Pollyanna Power, good works, and my ability to power or dream my way through anything.

Why did John stay? I don't know. John's image had already sustained damage when he resigned from his pastorate. That took a lot of courage. He wasn't sure he wanted to stay in ministry anyway. So why stay with me?

I think the decision came down to the children. Neither of us trusted the other to raise our children well, but a custody battle wasn't something either of us wanted.

So we stayed.

Time passed.

We repaired our images and built new ministries. I learned to accept what I had and put away my longings for something more. Sometimes that looked like settling, other times I found contentment in this situation.

Does Hope Remain?

I tried desperately to save the life I knew. What I didn't realize was that I was slowly losing my soul.

I didn't really understand why I was so afraid of a life without the image. By this time I'd seen God at work in our family in miraculous ways. We went on to weather more storms and recover from greater losses. And still, neither of us trusted God with our carefully constructed and fearfully maintained image.

I had learned to trust God for his provision in crisis. I trusted God to always have a purpose for me. But I hadn't learned to trust him with the very heart of who I was—my person.

I knew God would feed me and lead me. I assured others that he would restore their souls, and I believed it for them. But I didn't think God could possibly care enough about me for me to dare to hope that he would restore my soul.

I remained fairly confident in the dream story I'd written for our happy ending. God healing our marriage was clearly an expectation of future good—such a miracle would provide for our children and give us a purpose. Surely a good God would want to preserve and purpose our marriage.

But the hope I carried after my visit to the attic shifted into resignation. My wounded heart viewed God's goodness with constraints toward myself and limited his love for me to something I could measure.

Your Turn

What are some flashbulb moments in your life?

Henry Blackaby calls these turning points a crisis of belief because they call into question what we believe about ourselves, God, and the world. When our belief is tested, the outcome directs our next steps. How has a flashbulb moment changed your thinking and determined your direction?

Chapter Six

People Who Stay

"Don't run from trouble. Take it full-face. The "worst" is never the worst. Why? Because the Master won't ever walk out and fail to return," Lamentations 3:30-31 The Message.

In my Texas hometown, tornadoes were our main weather threat. When a warning came, you stayed in place until the storm passed. Not at all like hurricanes.

One week after I moved to New Orleans, Hurricane Elena made her erratic path toward us.

On that Labor Day weekend, I was scheduled to attend an orientation for my Speech Pathology classes at LSU-Medical Center. John and I were newly engaged with plans to leave town the next day, pick up his sister in Mobile, Alabama, and visit his family in Macon, Georgia.

I noticed the heavy traffic in the westbound lanes as I headed East on the interstate. I wondered if it was always at a standstill at this time of day, and made a note-to-self to plan ahead in the future.

At the school, the hallways were in chaos. I stopped someone who looked like she had some authority and asked where my class was meeting.

"Class is cancelled," she said. "There's a hurricane coming."

I was disappointed. Class was already starting a week later than originally scheduled.

Wanting to make the most of my trip downtown, I asked, "Can you tell me where the bookstore is? I haven't bought my books yet."

"Honey," she enunciated slowly, "there's a hurricane coming. We're all leaving. You need to get out of town."

This was my first experience with an approaching hurricane. But it wasn't my last.

We did not stay in New Orleans for Hurricane Katrina in 2005. We drove to Pearlington, Mississippi, where the eye of the storm passed right over us. Our house flooded and we lost many of our worldly possessions. We grew closer as a family and as a community during the aftermath of that storm.

Hope Tested

A good friend who experienced similar losses that year led me to Psalm 27:13-14. "I would have despaired unless I had believed that I would see the goodness of the Lord in the land of the living. Wait for the Lord; Be strong and let your heart take courage; Yes, wait for the Lord."

Judi printed those on cards and shared them with others during that year and in the years ahead. She treasured the words in her heart and I came to treasure them in mine as well.

Over the next two decades, my friend and I experienced much worse tragedies than our Katrina losses. We prayed for our loved ones together and waited for our Lord to heal them. Amid unspeakable losses—my husband and her son among them—we encouraged each other to trust the healing we'd prayed for had come even when it was beyond our sight.

She spoke these verses over me and prayed for me to be strong and take courage. Other times, I was the one to strengthen and encourage her. We saw God's goodness. When we couldn't see it, we learned to rest in knowing and trusting that He is good.

Hope in the goodness of God takes a beating when God's mercy seems fierce, and His answers aren't what we wanted them to be. This hope is tested. And it stands.

After we married, John and I rarely evacuated for a storm. We had a gas stove and a generator to run the fridge, freezer, and other necessities of life. He hated sitting still in traffic. He disliked being unable to return home to clean up when he was ready.

We were people who stayed.

Eighteen Years

We took the same approach to our marriage that we did to hurricanes.

After John left the counseling center, we relocated back to New Orleans. It would be our home together for the next eighteen years and then another six for me alone.

I hoped the relocation would give us a fresh start. But I soon learned that you never leave your troubles behind. No matter where you run, you're always there.

We were our own worst enemies.

John's sexual addiction continued to manifest itself in various ways over the rest of our life together.

At times, I felt hopeful. We started working through the books we'd purchased for our fix-it-ourselves plan. But when his response to *His Needs, Her Needs* was that he had no needs, I realized the books weren't going to fix us.

At times we seemed to make progress and grew closer. We talked more openly. We took anniversary trips and went to the theater. We had coffee together in the mornings, and he sometimes brought lunch to me at work. We seemed to enjoy each other. Then I would discover a letter, a picture, or a pop-up on a screen. Once more he was acting out his addiction.

My pattern was to spiral through a season of despair with occasional bursts of anger, convinced nothing would ever change except to get worse.

I buried myself in reading, watching TV, and shopping. I joined multilevel marketing businesses and threw myself into selling baskets, make-up, or essential oils.

I doubted John told me the truth about our finances. Instead of limiting my spending just in case, I decided to take his assurances at face value and assume we had plenty to fund whatever I was into at the moment.

Then one of us would be convicted by a sermon we heard or a Bible study we were doing, and we'd start working on our marriage. We'd be hopeful again. For a season.

In between hope and despair, sometimes I exercised *conscious cluelessness.* I pretended to myself we were okay. I avoided situations where I might see something I didn't want to see. We moved through life adjacent to one another—the same home and the same family—but never really together.

Wilderness Years

For these twenty wilderness years, we moved in and out of states of existence. Never leaving. Always staying. But never living in the abundance of life God promises his children.

We seldom fought.

John would not fight. He wrote in one of his journals that I wanted to fight, and he refused to indulge me. If I'd known his thoughts, I would have begged him to fight—not against me, but with me—for our marriage.

In the book of Exodus, God rescued his people from centuries of slavery in Egypt. He led them through the wilderness to a "land of milk and honey" he promised to give them. But the book of Numbers tells us that when they got to the promised land, the people who lived there seemed like giants to them. They were too afraid to go in and fight for the land. They ended up staying in the wilderness for forty years because they didn't trust God's promise.

Looking back, it's hard to believe we let our wilderness years continue for so long. I can't rule out apathy as a reason—there were times when we just drifted.

Christians typically view wilderness experiences as an opportunity for transformation. I believe John and I grew in some areas of life. But transformation happens when we do the hard work of admitting and wrestling with our sin.

I don't believe we will experience victory over sin in our life or the sickness it brings if we don't stand and fight. Staying isn't the same as standing. The Holy Spirit gives the strength needed to stand. And it's in the standing that we develop a hope that remains. Sometimes we have to fall apart—dismantle and release the idol—to be rebuilt. John and I didn't fight. We averted our eyes.

Glimmer of Hope

Each time I was ready to give up, something happened to give me a glimmer of hope. We'd have a good conversation. We'd weather a storm or get through a crisis with the kids together. I saw a glimpse of the partnership I longed for.

That glimpse, that glimmer of hope, was enough to make me stay. But it wasn't enough to make me fight.

During a hopeful season, I talked about my hope for healing and future ministry. John seemed to listen. I told myself he agreed.

And then I waited for him to do something about it. In my mind, I did what a good wife should do. I waited for my husband to take the lead.

My passivity didn't look anything like the love described in the Bible. Among other things, biblical love is patient and kind, and does not insist on its own way. Biblical love rejoices in the truth. It "bears all things, believes all things, hopes all things, endures all things" according to 1 Corinthians 13:4-7.

I ignored my responsibility for my own relationship with God and others. I waited for someone else to demolish my idols.

My passivity didn't keep me from longing. Like the Israelites at the edge of the Promised Land, I could see the fruitfulness and abundance possible in a life of light and truth. But the obstacles to overcome seemed too big, and I felt too small.

We were people who stayed in the wilderness. Over yonder just out of reach, sat the promised land. We didn't give up on our marriage, but we didn't fight for it, either. We wandered in the wilderness.

Complacency

Determined to maintain our image, we had to keep people at a distance. Even our closest friends did not know our struggles. John and

I each occasionally had accountability partners. Even with them, we only got so close before the wall went up to protect our image.

Both of us offered pastoral counsel to people struggling with the same challenges we were. But we didn't share our struggles. We gave counsel we believed to be good, but it was counsel we didn't follow.

I got used to the life we lived. I wasn't happy or unhappy. I wasn't content or bitter. I was complacent.

Our kids and our ministries kept John and I together. We both enjoyed our children and our work. I appreciated the kind of father he was to our son and daughter. We supported the kids in school activities and at church. We chaperoned mission trips and camps. We led a class on parenting teenagers.

Once, we spoke on marriage at a Valentine's banquet. I have no idea what our audience thought but the experience felt horrible for me. Perhaps John was just as miserable because we never did that again.

Oasis Moments

Toward the end, we taught Bible classes together in the seminary's prison program. John was a great teacher. I was awed at his memory for details and ability to recount historical events. He rarely referred to notes as he taught. John was so winsome even our incarcerated students never lost interest.

For the first time in our marriage, John seemed to appreciate what I had to offer in ministry. One time he told me he clearly understood a concept for the first time when I explained it, although he'd heard and taught the same concept himself many times. Simple and not at all romantic, but such moments were an oasis, and I drank every drop of refreshment. I'd dreamed of ministering together, and we were. These exchanges were just enough to get me through harder times in between. We didn't make progress, but we survived.

I read somewhere that grief is like having a computer program running behind the scenes. You don't always notice, but your computer does not run at optimum capacity. The secret pain in our marriage constantly bogged me down. I learned to cope like someone copes with a missing limb. It wasn't ideal, but I adapted and managed.

We stayed, but we never made the most of our staying. In the stories and teachings of the Bible, God urges his children to be courageous and stand firm.

We stayed, but we didn't stand.

We would not have a sustaining hope that remained through the storms as long as we saved our lives at the expense of our souls.

Amazingly, God chose to work through us anyway. We got to do some incredible ministry and saw results. Our children grew up to be people I like and respect.

I don't understand why God would show us such kindness when we lived a lie. I suppose that's grace.

But I'll always wonder what God could have done in and through us if we put our hope in him instead of our image.

Your Turn

When life gets tough the tough get going, takes on a new meaning when you need to decide whether to leave or stay in a difficult situation.

Have you had to make such a decision about a job, a team, or a relationship?

Do you have a particular bent toward going or staying?

What part do commitment, fear, image, safety, or other concerns play in your decisions?

Chapter Seven

Hope Lost

"Hope deferred makes the heart
sick," Proverbs 13:12 ESV.

"How is this anniversary different?" The week before what would have been my 30th wedding anniversary, my counselor asked the question.

"My husband's gone." I thought an answer was obvious.

"He is. But what were anniversaries like when he was here? Your marriage wasn't great," my counselor said. "So how does his absence make this one different?"

My answer was immediate. "There's no more hope."

Wedding Anniversary

Every year for twenty-nine years, on the anniversary of our wedding day, I hoped. Surely this would be the year. At last, everything would finally change for the better. This year we would go out to dinner. Maybe we would go away for the weekend. We would focus on us. We'd remember that something special drew us to each other. We would relive the day we loved wholeheartedly and promised to love forever.

If we remembered how we'd loved then, maybe we could love again now. We could demolish the image and confess our lies. We would get help and heal. We would love each other the way a husband and wife are supposed to love one another.

We'd emerge battle-worn and scarred, but older and wiser. We could become a shining example of how a marriage can survive and thrive after addiction and betrayal. And we could teach others how we had done it.

With God's help, of course.

The ministry would be better and more effective. God would take all the pain, the waiting, and even all the hiding. He'd work it together for our good and his glory.

I had begged God to do this work in us. I had believed he would. I had hoped he would.

I hoped.

Every year.

But this year, I wasn't hoping for anything.

Maybe that wasn't so bad. Every year I hoped and every year I felt disappointed. This year, I didn't hope and I would not be disappointed.

Emmaus Lesson

A while back, I went to church to procrastinate on writing this book.

Our lesson that night was from Luke 24:13-35. In the account of one of Jesus' appearances after his crucifixion and resurrection, two disciples are walking and talking about the death of Jesus. We know they were his followers because the story calls them disciples. They knew Jesus well.

Jesus shows up but they don't recognize him. He asks about their conversation, and they catch him up with the news of his own crucifixion.

Their feelings of disappointment and hopelessness are obvious. After they talk for a while, Jesus taught them. The story says he opened the Scriptures to them about himself. His teaching an expanded on what he taught them before he died. They don't recognize Jesus until they sit down to eat and he prays.

As soon as they realize this is Jesus, and are convinced of his resurrection, he leaves.

There I was, trying not to think about my book, and the two things hit me hard.

First, the disciples complained to their mysterious companion, "we had hoped that he was the one to redeem Israel. Yes, and besides all this, it is now the third day since these things happened," Luke 24:21, ESV.

My reaction to this verse had been, "Wake up, disciples. You're as bad as Lois Lane and Mary Jane Watson (I'm giving DC and Marvel Comics equal time here). How do you not recognize Jesus? You had hoped he was the one, and he was. The events didn't go exactly the way you expected it to happen. Get over your disappointment and see who's walking right beside you."

God's stories in the Bible are there to tell me about God and his ways. The characters are far from perfect, yet God loves and gives them purpose. I relate easier to characters who mess up. Their stories help me see how God loves and gives me a purpose. Maybe, I hope, he'll be as patient with me as he was with these two guys who didn't even recognize Jesus.

No Clue

I no longer call the disciples who met Jesus on the road to Emmaus clueless. I lamented to God using their very same words.

I had hoped.

I grieved over a hope I thought was lost when I was walking in its fulfillment.

I had hoped that God would heal, restore, and use us.

Naked and alone in the rubble of our image, I thought that hope was lost and I was alone. But hope wasn't lost and I was not alone. I needed to recognize Jesus walking right beside me.

My counselor helped wake me up. Together, we examined each piece of rubble from my shattered image. Over time, God identified the expectations I'd built on positive thinking, romantic imagination, legalistic self-righteousness, and self-sufficiency.

God showed me what hope I'd placed in eternal truths about him, his character, and his ways.

He showed me the difference between the image I'd manufactured and my identity in Christ.

I didn't toss aside the things I'd put my expectations in:

- I'm still a positive thinker. I like that about me.

- I'm okay with loving a good love story.

- My walk with Jesus is deeply enriched by the practice of spiritual disciplines.

- I worked hard to adopt some of John's can-do attitude. I learned fearless confidence goes a long way when I'm living in an RV (more on that later).

- I will always be a dreamer. I'm learning not to dream while driving, but I'll never stop dreaming.

Nothing I built into my image was inherently bad. But when I tried to cover my sin, my struggles, and myself, the good things became a false image. The image became a life I wanted to preserve and protect. I lost sight of the abundant life God promised.

When I put my hope in the image, that image became an idol. I trusted the image I created rather than the God who created me. I expected the image to accomplish what I wanted—a meaningful life of love and respect. Sometimes, it did. But anything I got out of my idol did not last. The hope I put in my image did not stand the test of time. Hope placed in God does remain. Hope in God does not disappoint.

That said, was there anything I hoped for during those years that was fulfilled?

- I hoped that the image would be gone. It is. We didn't demolish it ourselves. God, in his fierce mercy, demolished it for us.

- I hoped that John would be healed. He is. He's at home with Jesus and not suffering anymore from addiction or depression.

- I hoped we would get help. I have. I cannot say enough about Professional Christian Counseling and the power of community.

- I hoped we would tell our story to help others with similar struggles. I'm doing that. I speak at churches and mental health conferences. I write. I answer calls and texts, and sit one-on-one with people who hear my story and feel they can share theirs.

- I hoped we'd be an example of how to save a marriage after unfaithfulness. I'm not. But I can give caution. Our marriage is a warning.

- I hoped that John and I would love each other. That didn't happen. But I have a God who sees the very heart of me and loves me well.

- I hoped God would work everything for good. He did.

I hoped. I stayed because I hoped.

Does the fact that much of my hope was in the wrong things mean I shouldn't have stayed in my marriage? I can't say. I regret some reasons I stayed, but I don't regret that decision.

Does my experience indicate that someone in a similar situation should stay? I can't say that either. I don't know your life. I don't know what sort of physical or mental danger you or your children may be in. I don't know if God is working things out for you where you are, or if he's working out plans for you in another place.

I can't tell you if you should stay or go. I can only tell you that you should definitely remain in Christ. Listen to him, and his Spirit will guide you. Read the Bible and let God's words remain in you. Find a supportive church community and plug in.

Suicide shattered my dreams for the family I longed to have. But John's death did not destroy my hope. For a minute or two—a season of waiting and watching—I thought it had. But God restored me to himself, his son, his word, and his community.

Eventually, I rediscovered the remnant of hope that remained.

Your Turn

"I had hoped" is such a sad little phrase. Can you think of a time that you had hoped, and hoped, and hoped some more—only to have that hope disappointed? Another phrase turns hope lost into hope found. "But God." I've been circling, "But God" everywhere I find the words in my Bible. Here are a few examples:

With man this is impossible, but with God all things are possible, Matthew 19:26.

You intended to harm me, but God intended it for good, Genesis 50:20.

My flesh and my heart may fail, but God is the strength of my heart and my portion forever, Psalm 73:26.

Would you like to practice laying a "but God" alongside your lost hope? I'll do the first one, then you do the rest:

I had hoped God would heal my marriage, but God healed my husband, and restored my soul.

I had hoped ____,
but God ____.

I had hoped ____,
but God ____.

I had hoped ____,
but God ____.

Chapter Eight

Shameless Hope

"Therefore, since we have been justified through faith, we have peace with God through our Lord Jesus Christ, through whom we have gained access by faith into this grace in which we now stand. And we boast in the hope of the glory of God. Not only so, but we also glory in our sufferings, because we know that suffering produces perseverance; perseverance, character; and character, hope. And hope does not put us to shame, because God's love has been poured out into our hearts through the Holy Spirit, who has been given to us," Romans 5:1-5.

What should I expect on the first Sunday after the funeral?

As I went to church my insides churned with a strange mix of dread and eager anticipation. Eager to see my people, I didn't look forward to their looks of pity.

I had hoped for nearly 30 years. Now my husband was dead, and everyone knew how I foolishly stayed and waited. I felt ashamed of my loss, ashamed I stayed, and ashamed of my hope.

Would my church family be angry with me for my part in hiding John's addiction? How would they respond to my lack of honesty?

What I dreaded most was being judged. I struggled with the thought that John's addiction and his suicide were my fault. I blamed myself. I was sure others blamed me, too. Did people think I was stupid and weak for staying? Was I foolish for continuing to hope against hope?

I longed for the comfort of hiding myself in my familiar image. Now that image was demolished, I wanted something to wrap around my nakedness and hide me from the stares.

For the most part, my fears were unrealized. People didn't stare, and the friends who spoke with me gave nothing but compassion, love, and care.

But two people said things that made me cringe.

Their comments had the power to hurt because they confirmed questions I'd asked myself. Had there been red flags about his addiction in John's interactions with church members? What had made my husband look outside our marriage?

Neither of the two had answers to my questions. They seemed to be wondering, just like I was. Unfortunately, they did their wondering out loud.

I'm convinced that neither person spoke with an intent to harm. I've tried to believe they spoke with the intent to help, but if that's the case, they didn't think it through. Regardless of their intent, I felt shame.

In response, I fell back on old hope habits. Smiling, thinking positive thoughts, and shifting the spotlight to someone else's needs were enough to get me through the moment. Once I found a seat and caught my breath, I even managed to laugh about how awkward the interaction had felt.

Later, when I was alone with my thoughts, shame returned like a tidal wave. My old strategies had worked in the moment, but shame isn't momentary. Shame takes embarrassment and humiliation to a whole new level. Well beyond the embarrassment of having done something bad shame says, "You're a bad person."

Deeply seated shame can lead to despair. And despair can kill hope that's based on anything I can do on my own.I had a deeply seated shame. I also had a hope that was securely based on God's goodness, Jesus' love, and the Holy Spirit's power.

I just needed to find it.

I Am That Woman

I had used the phrase, "I don't want to be that woman," often enough that my counselor eventually asked, "Who is this woman you don't want to be, and why do you think you're better than her?"

Ouch. That may have been one of those counseling days when I got a speeding ticket driving back home because I was so mad at my counselor.

"Who is this woman?"

She's naked. She's ashamed. She's pathetic. She's pitiful.

"Why do you think you're better than her?"

I don't. I'm not. How could I be? I am her.

I am Naomi in the biblical book of Ruth—whose husband moved her to a foreign land. Then he died. Then her sons died, too. She was left to fend for herself with two foreign daughters-in-law. Bitter, hopeless, and alone, she told her daughters-in-law, "You're better off without me. God himself is against me."

I am Leah whose story starts in the 29th chapter of the book of Genesis—her father tricked her husband, Jacob, into marrying her. Unloved, Leah was constantly pitted against her prettier sister—who her husband did love and also married. Leah used bribery and her ability to bear sons to manipulate her sister and get Jacob into her bed. She was sure she could make him love her.

I am Christi, who spent thirty years in a wilderness of a marriage because I thought someday my husband would turn back to me, see me, and love me. I thought if I did enough for God, he would give me the desires of my heart.

I had no respect for Naomi or Leah, and I had no respect for myself.

Words of Truth

Once I spoke my shame aloud, confessing it first to God and then to my counselor, shame lost its power over me. I identified the lies I heard and believed in each story. I laid the lies next to the words of truth God said about Naomi, Leah, and me.

A few months into this struggle with God, I went on a snowy retreat in Idaho. A new friend asked if she could pray a passage of Scripture over me.When I agreed, she laid her hands on my shoulders and read from Isaiah 54, starting in verse four.

These verses were written as a promise from God to Israel, not to me. But as my friend prayed the words over me, I saw the goodness of God in them and felt the deep comfort his love poured into my heart.

Fear not, for you will not be ashamed; be not confounded, for you will not be disgraced; for you will forget the shame of your youth, and the reproach of your widowhood you will remember no more. For your Maker is your husband, the Lord of hosts is his name; and the Holy One of Israel is your Redeemer, the God of the whole earth he is called. For the Lord has called you like a wife deserted and grieved in spirit, like a wife of youth when she is cast off, says your God. For a brief moment I deserted you, but with great compassion I will gather you. In overflowing anger for a moment I hid my face from you, but with everlasting love I will have compassion on you," says the Lord, your Redeemer. For the mountains may depart and the hills be removed, but my steadfast love shall not depart from you, and my covenant of peace shall not be removed," says the Lord, who has compassion on you. — Isaiah 54:4-10 ESV.

New Season

As I received Father God's love and compassion, I felt my fear and shame subside. I asked God for wisdom in my confusion, courage in my indecision, and his honor in the reproach of my widowhood.

I returned from that trip ready to embrace the names of Naomi, Leah, and *Widow* with an enthusiasm that led me into a new season of life. In the rubble of my demolished image I rejoiced to find the hope I searched for. The hope that wouldn't disappoint. The hope that would remain.

I had suffered and persevered. I had sinned. But I hadn't given up on God.

And God wove his character of love, joy, peace, patience, kindness, goodness, faithfulness, gentleness, and self-control in me. God's character at work in me gave a hope based entirely in him. It is a hope that will not disappoint or put me to shame.

Born from the rubble of suffering, this hope remains through the storm and beyond.

Your Turn

After John's death, I went to the bank to get answers about my financial situation.

The banker was not sympathetic. "Please don't tell me you were that woman who knew nothing about the finances."

Once again, I was that woman. And I was deeply ashamed.

I had hoped but to no good purpose.

Have you been ashamed of hope?

Take your shame and suffering through the cycle of Romans 5:4-5. "We know that suffering produces perseverance; perseverance, character; and character, hope. And hope does not put us to shame, because God's love has been poured out into our hearts."

What pain or sorrow have you suffered?

How did you persevere in the waiting?

What sort of character did God build in you as you waited? Are you more loving, joyful, peaceful, patient, kind, good, faithful, gentle, or self-controlled. Consider Galatians 5:22.

How has God shown you who he is and how he's poured out his love on you?

Each time you work a trial through this cycle, you will see God at work more clearly than the last time.

Chapter Nine

Woman in the Mirror

"Teach me your way, O Lord, that I may walk in your truth; unite my heart to fear your name. I give thanks to you, O Lord my God, with my whole heart, and I will glorify your name forever. For great is your steadfast love toward me; you have delivered my soul from the depths of Sheol," Psalm 86:11-13 ESV.

For a long time, I was so angry with John for suiciding that I didn't have much empathy for his struggles.

But God held up a mirror to show me the toll my inner battle with sin had taken on me. I am convinced that John's inner battle led to the deep depression and despair that eventually killed him.

I wonder if he ever cried out like the psalmist, "Oh God, unite my heart to fear your name!" I know I have.

A heart at war with itself is bound for destruction unless God unites it.

I never outgrew making rainbows. When the rainbows faded, I hammered good works onto my image to make it appear stronger.

At church I learned about doing good works including prayer, Bible study, and serving others. Lying and stealing were bad works to be avoided. For this girl building her image, having a checklist of works was handy.

Obey mom and dad. Check this task off the list and nail the accomplishment to the image. Clear the table. Check off this task and add to my image. Go to church, sing in the choir, marry a preacher. Check. Check. Check. Grab the hammer, nail each one, and the image looks better and better.

Good works aren't bad. God has equipped us for works that he's uniquely prepared especially for each of us to do. Used correctly, spiritual practices like Bible study, prayer, and service discipline our minds. They help us know God better and draw near to him. Offered sincerely to God, they can be acts of worship.

But, when I put works on a checklist or nailed them to an image I created for myself, they lost their value. My works became an obstacle between me and God because my hope rested in being good enough because I did enough. Rather than hope in God, I hoped in my performance.

I hid behind my attitude and actions. But reliance on myself couldn't sustain a hope that would remain. God's grace, not my performance, is the only real solution to hopelessness. But, before I embraced my need for grace, I had to acknowledge my sin problem.

Nakedness, Sin, and Shame

Sin is choosing our way instead of God's.

The Bible says we all sin, and that's why things are not the way they should be in the world and in our lives. There's war, oppression, poverty, disease, and other crimes of one person against another. This mess is the result of sin in this world.

The Bible tells how God handled sin the first time it happened. The account begins in chapter one of the first book in the Bible titled Genesis. God created a man and a woman, Adam and Eve, and put them in the beautiful and fruitful Garden of Eden. God told them they could eat anything except the fruit that grew on one specific tree.

Life was abundant and good. The man and woman had plenty to eat and led satisfying lives. They were naked but were not afraid to be seen. They walked and talked every day with God.

Then Adam and Eve chose to eat the forbidden fruit. By choosing to go against God's instructions, they sinned.

Everything changed. For the first time, they were ashamed of their nakedness. Their trust-filled relationship with God was destroyed by a new emotion; fear. Adam and Eve tried to cover their shame by sewing fig leaves into clothing to cover their bodies. And they hid themselves from God.

When God found them, Adam and Eve confessed what they had done. God said their actions had destroyed the simplicity of life in the garden and they would have to leave. Their relationships with God, with each other, and the world they lived in became complicated. Adam and Eve would now be at odds with God and his good creation.

Sin distorts and complicates the simplicity of all the good God established.

A Future and Hope

After describing what they lost because of their sin, God showed how much he still loved Adam and Eve. God gave them a new covering, a lasting one that he made himself from animal skins. He promised redemption, a future, and a hope.

There are multiple layers of meaning in this story. God's character, justice, and grace are evident alongside his love and mercy.

Adam and Eve tried to cover what they had done and hide from God. Their fig leaves couldn't begin to do what God's covering accomplished. The same story happens over and over. God loves his people. His people sin. They suffer and cry out to God. He loves them still. That's grace.

Then Jesus came, and we see grace at its best in the story of his earthly life, death, and resurrection.

I learned about grace the same time I learned about works. I was taught that even if I built the most glorious image, and covered it with works, my image would never make me good.

You've probably caught onto this by now, but I'm a Jesus person—a Christian. That means I confessed with my mouth Jesus is my Lord, and believed God raised Jesus from the dead.

I accepted that something is terribly wrong in the world and in me because of sin. I confessed I can't fix what is wrong and I want to be saved from it. I believe Jesus is the only one who can save me because he alone lived the pure life and died the death that sin demands. He alone defeated death when he rose to life again.

Because of Grace

I call him my Lord and my Savior because he died for me so I could be raised like him. I know my body will die. But I have hope that I will live forever with God.

That's grace.

And because of grace—even though I still live in a world that's messed up by sin—I get to live in the simplicity and abundance of walking with God. Every single day.

Because of grace, my hope is in Jesus and in him alone.

So why, after I received his grace, did I continue to put hope in an image made of good works?

Because I complicated the simplicity of what God made. I fully understood and believed God's grace was enough to save me and reconcile me with God. I received that grace with great joy.

Yet, my hope for an abundant life remained wrapped in what I thought people thought of me. I wanted to impress. I wanted to be admired.

So I kept adding on works. I was as ridiculous as Adam and Eve would have been if they'd kept wearing fig leaves after God covered them with animal skins. I lived as if I wore a raggedy bathrobe over a ballgown. I hid all the wrong things.

Works Alone Hide Grace

I made for myself an image of works, and my self-made image is what showed. Anyone impressed by my good works missed God's grace at work in me.

When grace gets missed, hope gets misplaced. Lives that don't lead people to a hope in Jesus and his grace, will eventually lead them away from him.

The Bible emphasizes the weaknesses of the people whose stories it tells. Some people who God led to do great things were murderers, adulterers, and liars. They doubted God, complained about him, and even made their own gods to worship in place of him.

Peter's story leaves me shaking my head in disbelief. He lived day in and day out with Jesus. He was the first to say of Jesus, "You are the Christ, the Son of the Living God." But when Jesus was arrested, Peter was so afraid for himself that he denied he even knew Jesus. When Peter realized what he'd done, he wept bitterly.

The Apostle Paul is my go-to person for practical teaching about how to abide in Christ and live by the Spirit. But in the letters he wrote, he openly shared his personal struggle with sin and his angst over what speaking hard truths sometimes did to his relationships.

God wrote the biblical stories in a way that showed the weaknesses of his followers so that we could see the strength of his grace. For others to see the glory of God's grace at work in me, they must see my desperate need for grace. It is impossible to reflect God's grace and impress people with my works at the same time.

Works Alone Hide Sin

The works I built into my image didn't hide my sin from God, but they did sometimes hide it from me. I believed the image. I built a convincing image and ignored my sin.

Our sin is covered by grace. Our relationship with God is restored when we believe. But his instructions for life aren't arbitrary. They are good and equip us to live in day-to-day relationships with God, other people, and with creation.

If I live my own way, none of my relationships will be right. I may be okay with God because Jesus covered the penalty of death for my sin. But sin can still wreak havoc in my life.

God gives us everything we need to defeat sin in our day-to-day lives. However, we cannot confront what we cannot see. We have to bring our sin into the light.

When I slapped an image made of works over my sinful thoughts and actions, I isolated my sin in darkness. I hid my sin away from the healing that would only come through exposure to the light of truth. It was vital that I looked honestly at the woman in the mirror.

What were my thoughts and behavior and how did these agree with Scripture?

Sin doesn't die in darkness. It grows.

The writer of Psalms confessed, "When I kept silent, my bones wasted away through my groaning all day long," Psalm 32:3, ESV.

Hidden sin that becomes secret sin eats away at us from the inside out.

Even when I acknowledged that the life I'd built was a false image, I excused it as a necessity to hide John's struggles. I lied to myself, saying, "I would gladly demolish this image if I had the choice." I convinced myself the image was there to hide John's story, and only he could choose to demolish it. This may have been partially true, but the image hid my sin, too.

Hidden behind the image was bitterness toward my husband. Passivity, manipulation, and bursts of anger were just a few unhealthy ways I developed of relating to John, others, and God.

I was proud of the false image I built but protecting it required I live a lie. The image became my idol, and the time and energy I spent maintaining the untruth became worship. The sins of pride, lying, and idol worship are at the top of every biblical list of things God hates.

My image didn't cover or cleanse my sin. It only hid it.

Works Alone Displace Confession

Confession is one of the most powerful weapons we have against sin. When we confess our sin to God, he's faithful. He forgives our sin, he cleanses our hearts, and he heals us from sin.

I worked through dozens of Bible study books and journals before and during my marriage. Early on, I wanted God to show me my sin and his ways.I regularly prayed Psalm 139:23-24, "Search me, O God, and know my heart. Try me and know my thoughts. And see if there be any grievous way in me, and lead me in the way everlasting."

In later years, hiding my weaknesses and failures was a life habit and heart searches were rare. When I asked God to show me my sin, he shined his light of truth into the darkness behind my image. And I wasn't ready for him to clean up the mess.

Good works had displaced confession and my longing for a grace-filled, abundant life. I didn't want God to look at my heart, and I certainly couldn't let other people see it. I wouldn't let anyone come alongside to strengthen, encourage, or pray for me because I couldn't invite them to see behind the image. I missed out on the cleansing power of confession to God and the healing power of confession and prayer with others.

I taught classes on prayer, led prayer events, and prayed regularly for friends, family, church, my city, and the world. But I had no one to pray for the painful struggles in my marriage because I did not feel free to be honest.

A life without confession is dangerous. It was destroying me. It eventually took my husband's life.

War Within

I was at war within. The old me, driven by the need to impress, fought the new me, saved by grace and guided by the Holy Spirit who lives inside.Paul wrote about this struggle between the old self and the new person we are in Christ. He complained that he often did what he did not want to do and did not do what he wanted to do.

I can relate. I cannot count the number of times I've had words clamoring in my brain to be spoken but told myself, "I am not going to say that. It will hurt this relationship." A split second later, the words tumbled out of my mouth.

This struggle shows me why I can't just follow my heart or trust my conscience to do or say what is right. Both can be deceived.My heart can be convinced that what it wants is good. When I built my impressive image, I believed I could be a better mother, wife, teacher, and leader if people believed the image.

The Holy Spirit will always wage war with image building. I was at war with him and with myself.

I didn't recognize the extent of my own struggle with image until mine was demolished with John's death. So John and I never had the chance to talk about it.

I know he had accepted, believed, and received Jesus' sacrifice for his sin. He had a future hope.

Day After Day

Day to day, John struggled with sexual addiction. He expressed a desire to change but hesitated to seek help because if people knew his struggles, we'd lose the life and ministry we'd built.

Whenever I asked about his self-help strategy, John said he would fix his heart by reading the Bible. He planned to stay busy helping people so he wouldn't have time to sin. He worked hard, but his efforts did not work to keep him from acting on his addiction.

What's sad about the fear John and I had of being seen is everything we thought we would lose if people knew us was only image. There was more to our lives than that image. But we were so busy protecting the lie we couldn't see the rest.

Once the image was gone, and the dust had settled, I discovered many of our works were merely rubble to be swept away. Yet, the people we encouraged, God's Word we taught, and whatever we did in God's name with his strength remained.

Our hope in our image and our works was an insult to God's grace. He was patient with us, but he would not tolerate it forever. God demolished the image, and my hope in what I built was lost.

Your Turn

Has there been a time in your life when you felt naked and exposed?

If your world has come crashing down under the pressure of an illness, loss, or conflict, you saw some truth about yourself in the rubble. If you haven't yet endured suffering, think about what might be revealed if your moment was today.

What is there in your life that has or would withstand a storm or a fire?

Chapter Ten

Dance Lessons

"But do not overlook this one fact, beloved, that with the Lord one day is as a thousand years, and a thousand years as one day. The Lord is not slow to fulfill his promise as some count slowness, but is patient toward you, not wishing that any should perish, but that all should reach repentance. But the day of the Lord will come like a thief, and then the heavens will pass away with a roar, and the heavenly bodies will be burned up and dissolved, and the earth and the works that are done on it will be exposed," 2 Peter 3:8-10 ESV.

On the one-year anniversary of John's death, my children and I gathered to remember. My son agreed to participate only if I promised there would be no arts and crafts. I did try to comply. But I asked them to help me think through all the emotions we experienced over those initial months without their father. We wrote the name of each feeling on a smooth stone with a marker. Holding each stone, we felt its weight. Then we felt the weight of all of the stones together.

I kept those stones in a bag for several years. Finally, I scattered the stones with the names of the emotions we felt in a small flowerbed outside my new home. After several years in the sun and rain, the words gradually faded.

God was patient. He gave John and I numerous opportunities to demolish our image and choose light and truth. He let us stay in our wilderness for decades. But he will not tolerate our idols forever. And our image had become an idol. Eventually, it had to go.

Time doesn't heal all wounds, but time can dull the pain. In my experience, God creates beauty in the brokenness. People will talk to me because I am wounded, they will listen to me because they see my wounds. God forms brokenness into bridges. We are too quick to despise our wounds when our brokenness becomes the building blocks of bridges and connections.

Shared Struggles

I've lost count of the number of people who shared with me that they were unprepared for the struggles of marriage.

I'm not talking about leaving the toilet seat up, dirty socks on the floor, or snoring. We're always ready to prepare people for that sort of reality. But sharing our struggles with developing emotional, spiritual, and physical intimacy is a deeper challenge. Couples often enter marriage with hopes of being one with our spouse, only to run head-on into the barriers to that oneness. No matter how compatible two people may be, they are still two individual people.

Becoming one isn't always easy. We need a friend who has been down the same path before us, who can share their hard-earned wisdom or listen to our struggles with empathy. There seems to be no shortage of shared wisdom on the topics of parenting, financial issues, religion, and even politics. But when it comes to intimacy, my experience has been this is more of an issue for people who have grown up among people of faith than those outside the church or involved in another faith-based setting.

Why is this topic so hard to talk about openly and honestly? In my experience the difficulty arises because our expectations for intimacy live in the most tender and vulnerable part of us. Talking about romantic dreams feels too much like being naked.

If this topic makes you uncomfortable, I hope your discomfort won't keep you from reading, because this is important. I hope my willingness to share will encourage you to be less reticent.

Freedom and Healing

I'm not promoting unbridled sex talk. Believe me, I'd be as uncomfortable with that as anyone. But I'm open when I think it might be helpful. Let's face it, my nakedness has already been exposed. Once I'd worked through my initial shame I discovered freedom and healing in being vulnerable. Perhaps my openness will free you to examine what shaped your expectations and how that has impacted your hope. If this is an area of hopelessness, I hope you will find the courage to share with your spouse or a trusted friend who can encourage and pray for you. My healing began with a counselor who helped me gain perspective.

Expectations and hope are so closely linked that it's hard to discern one from the other. Here's how I differentiate them: Expectations are based on events or actions. For example, I expect someone to do something or I expect an event to happen. Hope is based on a person. For example, I hope in God because of who he is.

It's no spoiler to tell you that I'm certain the only trustworthy place to put our trust is in God. His goodness, love, and power ensure our hope will not be disappointed or put to shame.

God's Design

I entered marriage with pretty big expectations. So did John. Our expectations had been shaped by every romantic notion we'd had and every exposure to sexual intimacy. Romantic dreams of intimacy can fulfill our definition so far. God created marriage, and he called it good. He created the man, saw that he wasn't good alone, and created woman. In the beginning of the Bible book of Genesis, God told the first man and woman to be fruitful and multiply.

We can see God delights in delighting his children in that he made the process of fruitfulness something that not only builds intimacy and makes babies, but also brings pleasure. God made sex fun. God did not have to give us that. He could have made us fruitful in a much more practical and clinical way. But he didn't.

We make a mess when we claim this gift as a right. We feel entitled to sexual freedom that was not a part of God's design.

God intended his gift to be enjoyed in the context of marriage. We squander the gift when we feed our desires outside of God's plan, thinking that when we find our happily-ever-after person, we can put the gift back in the box and wrap it in wedding finery.

But we can't. The gift has become our master.

I think John came to this realization long before his addiction was publicly exposed. During a rare moment of vulnerability, John confessed, "I probably shouldn't have ever married."

By this time, any intimacy in our marriage had been destroyed. We talked relatively openly about that and I expressed a longing for restoration. In that moment, I think he knew what his addiction had stolen from me. I want to believe he was sorry for that.

John was addicted. He tried to master that addiction on his own but could not. Desire mastered him and eventually destroyed his hope for healing.

Could God have changed this? Absolutely. Many people fight and win over addiction. I've seen marriages healed and restored from the ravages of sexual addiction. Our marriage was not healed. To my great sorrow, my husband only became free from his addiction in death.

Joyous Expectation

As for me, I have no expectations that I will ever remarry. Unmarried, sexual intimacy is no longer an option for me. Not because I have no desire, but because I believe God's gift of sex is intended solely for marriage.

You may think, "But Christi. Surely God wants you to be happy?" I've heard this argument countless times. Sometimes I want to buy it. But I just can't.

I do believe God is a Good Father who delights in the delight of his children. He delights most in me when he and I are in a relationship. He loves showing me who he is and seeing me discover who I am in him. But he cannot delight in my sin because sin separates me from him.

And, you know what? Full disclosure? Sin sometimes does make me feel happy. In the moment.

But God knows such happiness is fleeting. And he delights in eternal joy much more than in happiness.

Desire will not be my master.

But is romance out for me? I don't think so. The romantic dreams I had about John and me may have died. But romance is alive and well.

Romance is defined using words like joyous expectation and mystery. Doesn't that sound a little bit like hope?

A Romantic

I'd like to suggest that God is romantic.

My hope now is rooted in a God that I know and trust. But there is much about him that remains a mystery to me. I rejoice when I find something new about how he thinks. God often surprises and delights me. I know he loves me. And I love him.

And guess what? He and I dance. He promises that he will turn ashes into beauty and mourning into dancing. And he does. Sometimes it's a slow dance, where I just lean into him. Other times it's more of a waltz, where I'm learning the discipline of staying in step with him—1-2-3, 1-2-3. And sometimes our dance is a joyous, freestyle celebration.

My hope in him is based on who I know him to be. I'm hopeful because I am confident God will always be the same. He will always be faithful to his character. And he will always be good.

That's not romance. That's trust. That's hope.

But I'm grateful that he's a God who will surprise and delight me on occasion. And I love dancing with him.

When our hope is based on the goodness of God instead of anything we ourselves can do, it will remain.

In the end, works, religion, legalism, and self-righteousness will always fail us.

God never fails.

Your Turn

Have you ever told a lie that became a way of life?

Maybe you presented yourself to the world as something you are not, or tried to hide something you are. Perhaps you created a lie to protect someone else. The lies we tell ourselves hold us captive.

What shackles are holding you back from living in freedom?

What weight and constraint keep you from dancing?

Chapter Eleven

Beyond Normal

"The thief comes only to steal and kill and destroy. I came that they may have life and have it abundantly," John 10:10 ESV.

I'm finding my new normal.

That's what people say after a destabilizing, routine-busting, life-changing event. Whether a welcoming new baby, relocating into a new home, or grieving the loss of a loved one—following the expected ceremonial markers of celebration or grief, we naturally look for equilibrium.

I survived the initial crisis. Finding balance in the chaos was next on the agenda. I learned that the new normal is new because something essential to the old is gone or something has been added that makes the old impossible.

We call it normal, because we long to wake up knowing what to expect in the day. To once again feel some familiarity and predictability.

Or do we? Is normal really life's highest aspiration?

Possibly the most common advice given to the newly bereaved is, "Don't make any big decisions for a year." I understand the reasoning behind the statement, but I don't think it's good advice.

My personal favorite unsolicited tip I received after loss is, "Drink lots of water." That's always wise, especially while smack-dab the center of a circle of grief.

A Moment Alone

People hover. While their actions were sweet and kind, every once in a while I needed a moment alone to breathe. Drinking plenty of water necessitated visits to the bathroom. No one followed me there. No one hovers over someone sitting on the throne. You're welcome.

The recommendation about not making big decisions is sensible. After a loss, it is common to not be in the best frame of mind to make more life changes. When the brain fog eventually clears, there may be regret over selling the house or quitting the job. Regret added to grief is not a good combination.

But, in the messy muddled middle of grief, every decision appears to be big. Deciding what to have for dinner can boggle the mind. That's why thoughtful people take casseroles to their grieving friends. They don't think buttery cornflakes baked on top of creamy chicken will fix the sorrow. But they hope the food will nurture body and soul and take a tiny bit of pressure off someone they love.

Often there are crucial decisions that must be made after a loss. Some decisions are huge and cannot wait a year. In those instances, listening to your grieving friend talk through available options is more helpful than dismissing the need to decide.

Finally, making a big decision—even just one—is empowering. One of the *feels* I felt after my husband's death was a sense of helplessness. There were so many things I didn't know, tasks I never before had to do, and so much existed outside of my control.

The first big decision I made as a widow felt hard and involved some angst. Once the choice was finalized, for the first time since John's death, I thought, "I'm going to get through this."

I needed to do something just so that I realized I could.

God is Able

After everything in my life had changed, my thinking shifted from "I know exactly what will happen today," to "I can make it through whatever happens today." With a hope that remains, my waking thought became, "I can, because I know God is able."

Some friends wondered if I planned to move back to Texas after John's death. I'd left my home state to marry him, so it made sense that I might go back now that he was gone. But I'd been in New Orleans for twenty-five years. I raised my children there. I couldn't imagine living anywhere else.

I decided to find my new normal in the place I'd come to consider my home. The house we lived in was a perk that came with John's job. My first order of business was to find a new place to live. No one rushed me, but I was in a hurry. I wanted the distance. I needed the autonomy.

God made a way, and within the year, I found a house where I could begin my new normal. Additional big changes occurred that year that required decisions. My parents sold their house in Texas and moved to a retirement community. I went on two mission trips to Ghana, one to China, and one to Alaska. Our church's missions were part of my job description, but even so, that was a lot in one year.

Major Decisions

My son graduated from college and began a new job on the same church staff where I worked. He moved into my home, started seminary, met the love of his life, married, and moved into his own address. Perhaps he had not heard the rule about no major decisions for the first year.

During this season, I experienced more loss. My best friend since high school and John's mother both passed away. The health of our living parents declined. My pastor/boss talked about retirement. My New Orleans best friends moved away. These were my call-in-crisis friends—the people I called when John died and the people I lived with when I wasn't quite ready to live alone. Their move wasn't a surprise, but it was a loss.

Each change, each moment of decision, and each loss was big on its own. Piled up and heaped together, these changes were life-impacting. I thank God for a wonderful counselor during that season and beyond. But even counseling was hard. Getting better can be hard work.

So. Life was new, but not at all normal.

I sensed that normal might not be God's plan for my future. And that wasn't necessarily a bad thing.

No One Likes Change

A colleague helped me get the word out about a change I was making at church. I could feel the censure in her eyes when she looked up from her computer and said, "You like change, don't you?"

I knew her opinion well on this topic but I teased her anyway. "Yeah, I do. Doesn't everyone?"

She shot back, "No one does." I'm pretty sure this time I saw pity in her eyes.

I know not everyone likes change. I'm not convinced that everyone hates it either.

But my coworker was right about me. I thrive on change.

As a child, I couldn't clean my room without rearranging it. I still frequently change the configuration of my RV. There isn't much you can do differently in seventy square feet of space. But I have fun trying.

My least favorite question is "What's your favorite...(insert just about anything)?" If pinned down, my choice is, "Variety." My favorite food? Variety. My favorite color? Variety. My favorite author, style of worship, movie, place to vacation? Variety.

I needed to tell you that, because before you go further, you need to know that the "not so normal" life God has called me to did not really require sacrifice.

Have you considered being not normal? Maybe not in the same way I am. If I tried to prescribe my lifestyle for anyone else, that would normalize my existence and I'd have to find another way of being abnormal.

Who Wants Normal?

Calling someone *Lord*—even when that someone is Jesus, the Son of the Living God—isn't normal.

Believing God raised someone from the dead isn't all that normal either.

The life of a follower and believer in Jesus is no ordinary life. It's not meant to be.

Jesus said in John 10:10, "I came that they may have life." He defeated death to give us that life. But there was more. Jesus said he came so we could have life. "And have it abundantly."

That wonderful word, *abundantly,* is found throughout the Bible. But I missed the abundance a lot. When I did see the word, I sometimes misunderstood, misappropriated, or mistook the meaning for something it isn't.

In the third chapter of his letter to the church at Ephesus, Paul prayed his readers would be rooted and grounded in Jesus' love, and they would comprehend how wide, and long, and high and deep that love is. Paul knew love like that was beyond their knowledge, yet he prayed they would know it. In his prayer for the Ephesians found in Ephesians 3:14-2, Paul includes the word abundantly. Paul prays with the confident expectation of hope because he knows he's praying to a God able to do more than he could ever think to ask.

Abundantly More

How much more?

Exceedingly, super-hyper-abundantly more.

The hyperbole there is Paul's, not mine. *Abundantly* must not have been a strong enough word for him, because Paul super-sized it.

I don't usually do this in print, because I know just enough Greek to get me into trouble, and I'm always afraid my seminary Greek professor will read what I've written and call me out on getting it wrong.

But what Paul did here seems really fun to me, and I want you to see what I see.

In the Greek language, the phrase looks like this:

δυναμένῳ ὑπὲρ πάντα ποιῆσαι ὑπὲρ ἐκπερισσοῦ

I think it's captured really well with the English translation, "able to do exceedingly abundantly above all." But there's something really fun in the Greek.

ἐκπερισσοῦ, a power word on its own, means superabundantly, exceedingly, or beyond measure. But Paul super-sizes that word with ὑπὲρ—which means over, beyond, or more than. He doesn't stop with one ὑπὲρ. He adds a second ὑπὲρ. He added two shots of espresso to an already highly caffeinated word.

By the way, ὑπὲρ sounds like hyper—and that's even more fun. Paul put abundance into hyperdrive.

Why is this meaningful?

I can never out-ask what God can do. He can always do more. How much more? More than my tiny little brain can even begin to imagine.

God is not ordinary. What he is able to do goes well beyond the stuff of normalcy.

So why would I, a person who holds a "confident expectation of future good based on the goodness of God, the love of Jesus, and the power of the Holy Spirit," ever want to settle for a normal life?

Jesus uses the word *abundantly* to describe his cousin, John the Baptist. This is not a guy anyone found on a poster promoting normal living. John the Baptist called the religious leaders of his day a brood of vipers. Speaking the bold truth to religious leaders and political leaders alike, John told King Herod his marriage to Herod's brother's wife was illegal.

Make a Difference

People ventured into the wilderness where John lived to hear him preach. Jesus asked some folks who'd gone to all that trouble to hear John, "Who did you go out to see?" His next questions were rhetorical, and the answers were assumed.

Did you go to see a reed shaken by the wind?

Nope. We went to see John.

Did you go to see a man dressed in soft, splendid clothing?

Nope. We went to see John.

Did you go to see a prophet?

Yep. John.

Just any old prophet?

Nope. We went to see John.

Yes, I tell you, and more than a prophet. (Luke 7:24-26).

When Jesus said John the Baptist was more than a prophet, he used our word. Abundantly.

John the Baptist is who Malachi wrote about 400 years before the events in Luke took place. Malachi wrote that when he came, the prophet would "turn the hearts of the fathers to their children, and the hearts of the children to their fathers."

He would make a difference. His life would matter.

I want to make a difference. I want my life to matter. And I'm convinced that in order to really matter, a life needs to be abundantly more than normal.

New Normal

It doesn't have to be anything that people would talk about. It doesn't have to be a life that would make it to one of those sensationalized news shows or even a local news feature that highlights someone doing something good.

An abundant life is full of whatever God has poured into it but maybe empty of what we tend to think of as normal.

After my husband's death, I stayed in New Orleans, serving on the staff of a local church for the next six years. God had a lot of healing to do in me and a lot for me to learn.

I noticed a few things about how my life took shape:

- my children grew up, married, and planted their lives six and ten hours from me in different directions

- my dad and John's passed away

- my aging mom began a descent into dementia. She also lived 10 hours away, in yet another direction.

- my life, touched by addiction and suicide, had given me a story with a message I felt passionate about, and was willing to share

- many of the people John and I had served with in New Orleans were now serving in churches across the country and around the world

This was my new normal.

I appreciated my church and my work there. I saw what God was doing in my city. I heard about what he was doing in other places Was it possible that I could go and see God's work in other places?

Your Turn

Did you have a normal life planned out for yourself?

What did that life look like?

Does the life you live look different from that plan?

Does different from normal seem less than normal to you?

Can you see God's super-hyper-abundance at work?

Compare these three states of normality in your life.
The normal I had planned:

The not-so-normal I live in now:

God's exceedingly, abundantly beyond normal in my life:

Chapter Twelve

Free To Go

"Now to him who is able to do far more abundantly than all that we ask or think, according to the power at work within us, to him be glory in the church and in Christ Jesus throughout all generations, forever and ever. Amen," Ephesians 3:20-21 ESV.

Writing to his friends in Rome, the Apostle Paul said something that I found deeply relevant in my life today.

"I thank God through Jesus for every one of you. People everywhere keep telling me about your lives of faith, and every time I hear them, I thank him. And God, whom I so love to worship and serve by spreading the good news of his Son, knows that every time I think of you in my prayers, which is practically all the time, I ask him to clear the way for me to come and see you. The longer this waiting goes on, the deeper the ache. I so want to be there to deliver God's gift in person and watch you grow stronger right before my eyes! But don't think I'm not expecting to get something out of this, too! You have as much to give me as I do to you," Romans 1:8-12 The Message.

I couldn't stop thinking about Paul's longing to go to this church and others to strengthen them and be mutually encouraged with them in their shared faith.I longed for the freedom to get in my car, go to my friends and family, strengthen and encourage them, and be encouraged by them.

Then I realized everything I had endured over the last thirty years, though it tore my heart to shreds, had served to give me the freedom to do what I longed to do.

I was free to go. I had no husband to consider or please. My children loved me but didn't need me. Well cared for, my mom only needed to see me occasionally and know I cared.

My heart and my concerns were mostly undivided. I didn't need to occupy a house or an office. And if occasionally I did have a need for either, I knew of several I could borrow for a day or two.

I had a choice. I could moan about my situation and wallow in the loneliness of being a widow. Or I could lean into the freedom of being on my own. I didn't choose to be a widow in my sixties. But I could certainly embrace it.

And that's what I did. Because I could.

God began to roll out a plan. I quit my job, got rid of most of my stuff, sold my house, bought an RV, and hit the road.

My ministry is *Come Alongside Ministries, Inc.* It's simple. It's just me. Coming alongside people in churches—wherever they are. If a church lets me know of a need, and I can get there in my RV, I'll come alongside.

Amazing Grace

I live in a Coachmen Beyond. It's a Class B motor home that I christened Amazing Grace.

I travel with three beanie babies I recovered from a box in the attic. My kids had collected them, but no longer wanted the stuffed toys. The collection was collecting dust so I gave them away. The beanies. Not the kids.

The three I kept include a baboon named Shirley, a frog named Gud Ness, and a pelican who goes by Murray C. They follow me all the days of my life. If you don't hear that pun right away, grab a Bible, find Psalm 23, and read aloud to hear the names of my mascots and what they do in verse nine. Pretend you're playing the game *Mad Gab*.

When a church invites me to come alongside in whatever way God is at work, I almost always say yes. That church becomes a destination, and I make plans to steer Amazing Grace in its direction.

I drive four to six hours each day with plenty of stops on the way to a destination. If I have a friend who lives in that direction, or am aware of a church with a need, or have heard from someone who follows my ministry and lives along the way, I contact them and ask if they'd like to be an official Stop Along the Way on this trip.

If that stop involves strengthening and encouraging our faith, it becomes as much a part of my come alongside journey as my destination.

Every trip is different. Each day, I begin the journey with hope that God will do something good with me that day. My working definition of a hope that remains is this: Hope is the confident expectation of future good based on the goodness of God, the love of Jesus, and the power of the Holy Spirit.

His Goodness

In his goodness, God brought me through a painful marriage and our relationship's tragic end. I'm on the other side. And I have a confident expectation of future good, because God is good, and he's here.

When I park Amazing Grace for the night, whether in a friend's driveway, a church parking lot, or an RV park, I lie down and rest in the love of my Lord Jesus, knowing I'm never really alone. Even when I get a little lonely in my camper van, I have this hope that remains, because he is with me. He loves me. And I love him.

Having abandoned Pollyanna Power, I carry on in the trustworthy power of the Holy Spirit.

I do get tired. Sometimes life is hard work. Because sin complicated our relationship with God's creation as explained in the first three chapters of Genesis, we labor in work that is hard. Admittedly, I embarked on this journey with none of the necessary skills needed for RV living.

Right now, I'm trying to understand PSI so I can take better care of my tires. I've wrestled with amps and wattages and converters and inverters. Sometimes when something mechanical or electrical blows a fuse in my brain or I make a nasty mess dumping my sewerage tanks, I complain to God, "Why can't I just have a normal life?"

On rare occasions, I've told him, "You know I need a man to do this stuff, right?"

He reminds me that I'm living a Beyond Normal life.

Freedom Dance

Before long, I change my tune from "Lord, I need a man" to "Man, I need you, Lord!" Followed by dancing my freedom dance.

By the way, isn't it fun that I bought an RV with a brand name—Coachmen Beyond—that goes so well with living an abundant life? I didn't even need to play with the languages to see that abundance is beyond normal.

My RV is pretty small, and you'd think it would be easy to keep things simple. There isn't space for anything but the essentials. Yet, I still complicate my life with things I don't need and burdens that aren't mine to carry. Releasing and letting go is a lifestyle I'm continually learning.

When I'm faced with a task that requires skills I don't have, I do what I watched my husband do for years. I search the internet for instructive videos, I try to read instructions, and I ask for help. With confident expectation, I pray for strength to move tightly screwed-on caps, loosen bolts, and separate magnets that are stuck together.

Sometimes the answer to that prayer is the strength to do the task, other times it's the humility I need to ask for help. Always, I know God is there, he's with me and for me, and I need him.

It's not a bad life. It's actually pretty awesome.

What About You?

I don't know the story God is writing in your life. I don't know what gives you hope or what brings you despair.

I know we're different, you and me. Our lives are different. Our joys are different. Our losses and trials are different. So is our freedom.

But there are a few ways that I think we are the same.

Jesus came so you could have life, and have it abundantly. You don't have to settle for covering your sin and shame with fig leaves. You don't have to settle for death. And you don't have to settle for normal.

If you haven't confessed Jesus as Lord, and can't quite believe God raised him from the dead—you can talk to God about it. You can find a Bible and read one of the books Jesus' disciples wrote about him. Called the Good News, the books of Matthew, Mark, Luke, or John each tell the same story about Jesus, but in different ways.

You can ask God to send to you a pastor or a friend who can talk with you about Jesus. Most churches would love to help you with that.

Or, you can contact me, if you'd prefer. Right now, the best way to do that is through the Come Alongside Ministries social media. Message me through Facebook or Instagram, or email through my website. I'd love to hear from you and will try to answer as quickly as I can.

God has a beyond normal in store for you. Look at what he's poured into your life. Look at what you care passionately about. Make a note of the verses in the Bible that stir your heart, the ones that you can't stop thinking about. And pray. He'll direct your steps. When he does, would you let me know? I'd love to hear from you.

Future Good

You have to embrace your beyond normal to live it. Maybe you're doing that already. Or maybe you're afraid for whatever reason. Maybe you're still longing for normal. Perhaps you feel a little hopeless. Pray. Ask God to show you what's holding you back and help you overcome it.

You have a hope that remains. It's possible that currently hope has gotten lost in the rubble of the other things you've put your hope in. Let God help you sort through the mess and show you the confident expectation of future good you have in his goodness, his love, and his power.

Thank you for reading my story. I hope and pray that God uses this experience to strengthen and encourage your faith. I know writing my story has done that for me.

I'd love to hear from you if you have questions or comments, or just want to share your story with me.

Reach out if you'd like to talk about your church or group being a stop or a destination for Come Alongside Ministries. I'll look at my calendar, and my map, and we can talk about possibilities.

I know one thing. If you know Jesus, I'll either see you on the journey, or at our journey's end.

Your Turn

New Orleans is below sea level. The area is shaped like a bowl, just waiting to hold all of the water from everywhere. The force of Hurricane Katrina broke the levees that keep the water out of New Orleans. As a result thousands of homes, businesses, and churches flooded.

One of those homes that flooded was ours.

For nearly a year, we were possession-free. We did not spend time and money caring for our stuff because we had no stuff. We vowed never to accumulate so many possessions again. We kept that vow until we didn't. As soon as we moved back, we populated our space once more with belongings.

When God pries something from our grasp, he frees our hands to receive his blessings.

God has somewhere for you to go—maybe into the next room, maybe across the street, maybe around the world. He may not want you to quit your job or sell your house. But he will ask you to let go of anything that holds you back.

Where do you long to be free to go?

Do you need to let go of possessions, privileges, anger, unforgiveness, or something else you're holding onto?

About the author

"Courageous. Vulnerable. Refreshing. A whole different animal."

Christi Gibson is an encourager, storyteller, and teacher.

Formed in Texas and shaped by New Orleans, during her third thirty-years of life, Christi travels in her RV, christened Amazing Grace. Home is whatever park, driveway, or parking lot where she stops in along the way.

A stranger to no one, Christi looks for a story to hear, read, or tell. Through *Come Alongside Ministries* she takes her love for story to retreats, conferences, and workshops—wherever people gather to be strengthened and encouraged.

She brings everything to the table—her years as a pastor's wife, seminary professor's wife, stay-at-home and working mom, her experience as a local church minister of connections, discipleship, and missions, a teacher in seminary and women's prisons, a church lady on Bourbon Street, and her M.Div in Biblical Studies from New Orleans Baptist Theological Seminary. Occasionally her training and experience as a Speech Pathologist is put to good use.

Most of all, Christi shares her pain and healing, failures and successes, strengths and weaknesses, as well as her odd sense of humor and spirit of adventure.

Other books by Christi include *Your Story Matters* and *Stir Up the Gift*

Connect with Christi Gibson through her social media.

https://comealongsideministries.com/

https://comealongsideministries.com/blog/

https://www.facebook.com/ComeAlongsideMinistries/

https://www.instagram.com/comealongsideministries/

christigibson@comealongsideministries.com